What's the BIG Idea?

What's the BIG Idea?

Tohby Riddle

PENGUIN|VIKING

To Sally, for her patience and support,
and for her ability to give feedback when awoken
by a night owl waving pieces of paper.

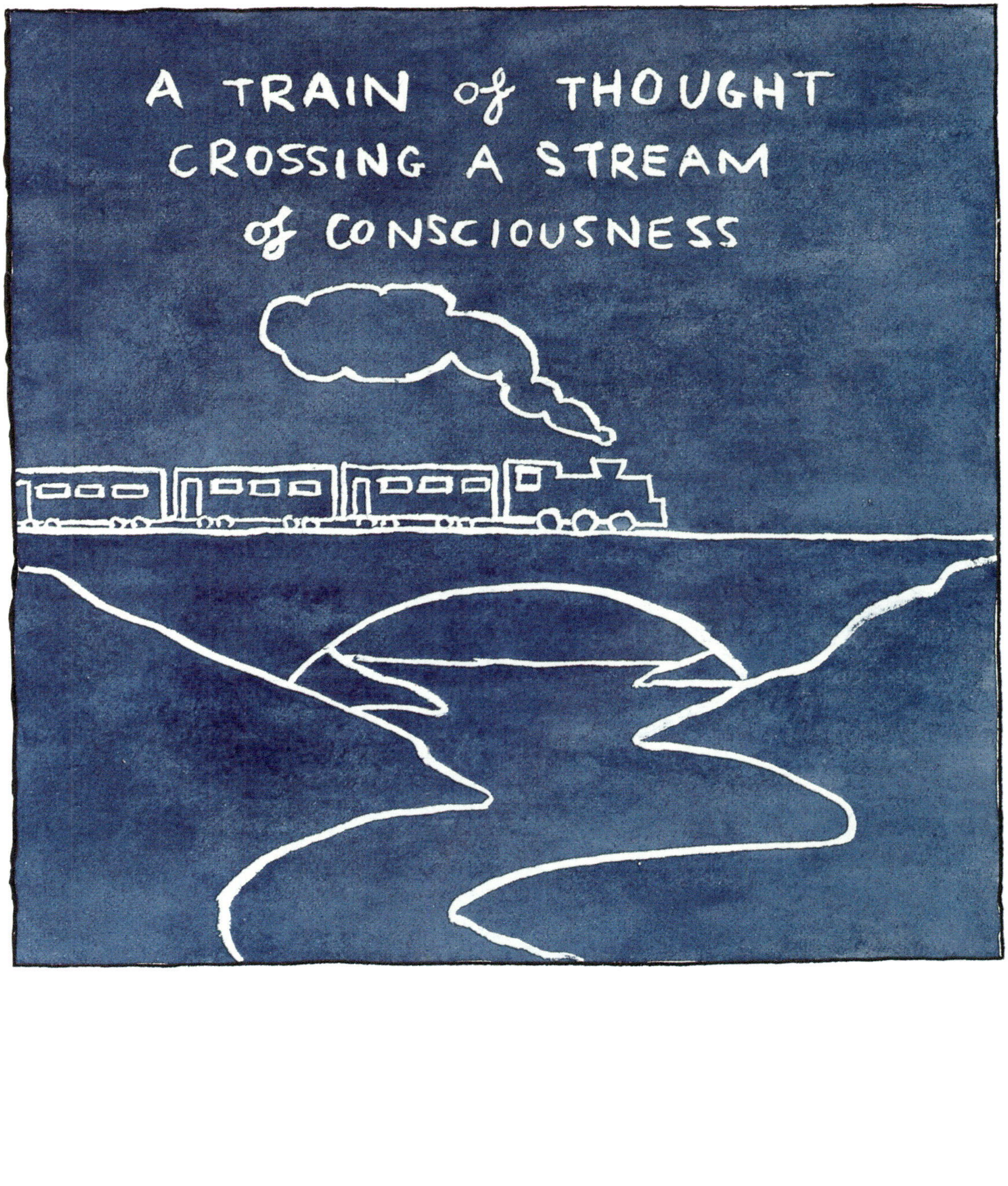
A TRAIN of THOUGHT
CROSSING A STREAM
of CONSCIOUSNESS

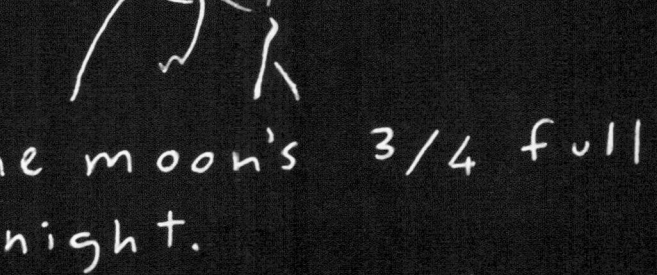

The moon's 3/4 full
tonight.
But something about it
isn't right...

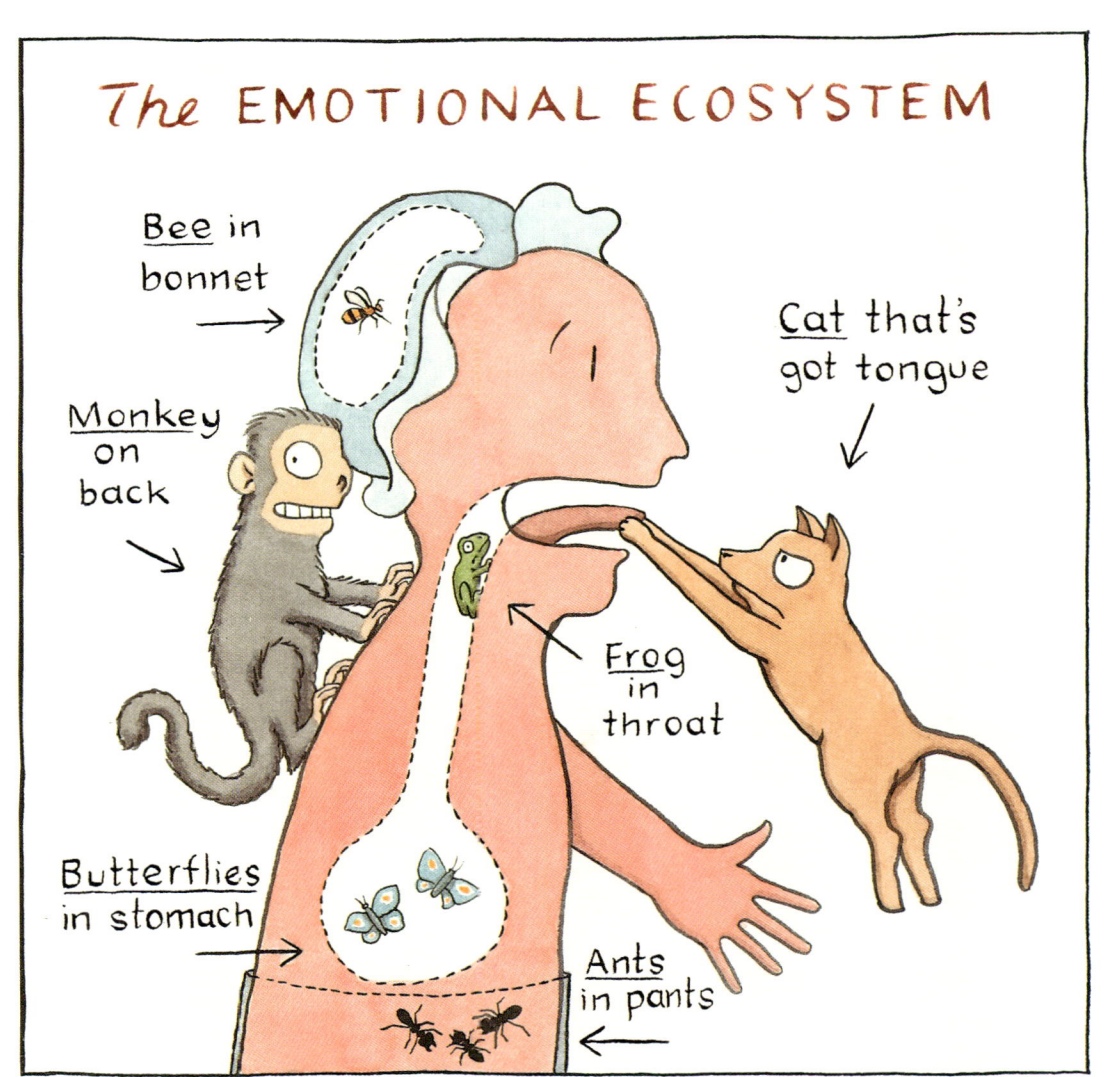

DOG OF THE WEEK

Buster is a 2-year-old male labrador who needs a family. He's good with children, loves walks, the films of Jacques Tati and Cuban cigars.

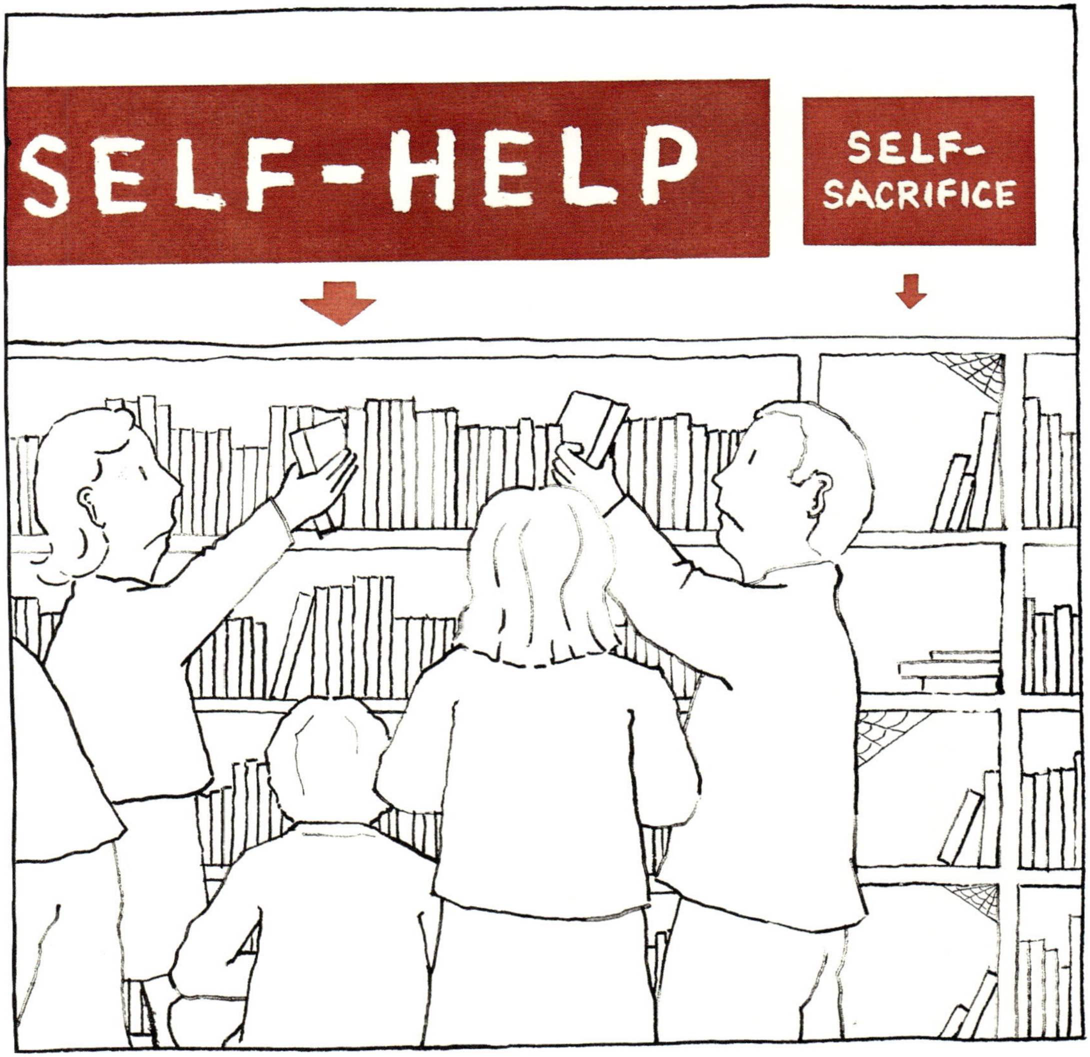
SELF-HELP
SELF-SACRIFICE

When I grow up I'm going to be an artist!

When I get some spare time I'm going to be an artist!

When I retire I'm going to be an artist

When I get off this life support system I'm going to be an artist

Yeah! I'll take up jogging and I'll get fit and lose weight and ... aaah, what's the point? I wonder what's on telly?

gung ho hum, *adj.* to vacillate rapidly between intense enthusiasm and total lack of interest.

The HERMETIC SEAL

NORMALLY I'M YELLOW

Normally I'm yellow

A colour bright and keen

But when I feel a little blue

I go a funny shade of green

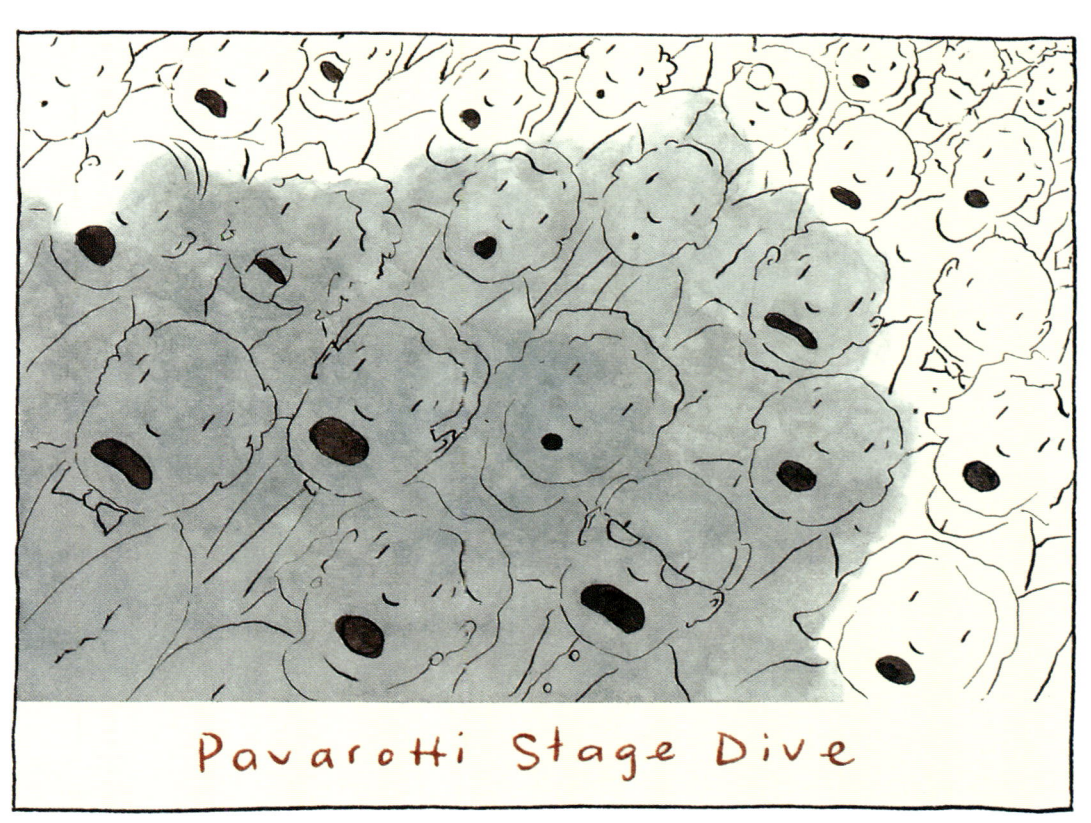

Pavarotti Stage Dive

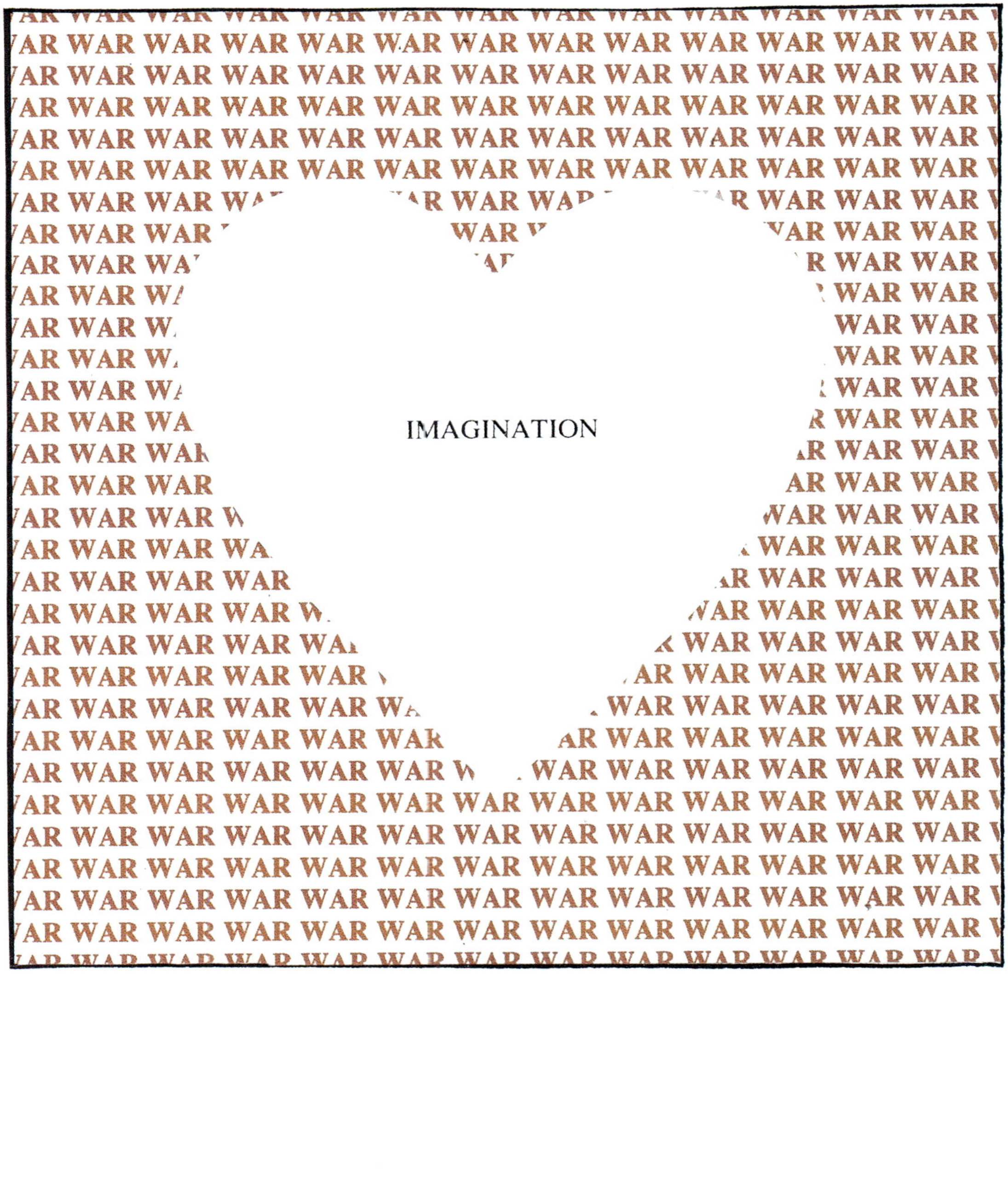
WAR
IMAGINATION

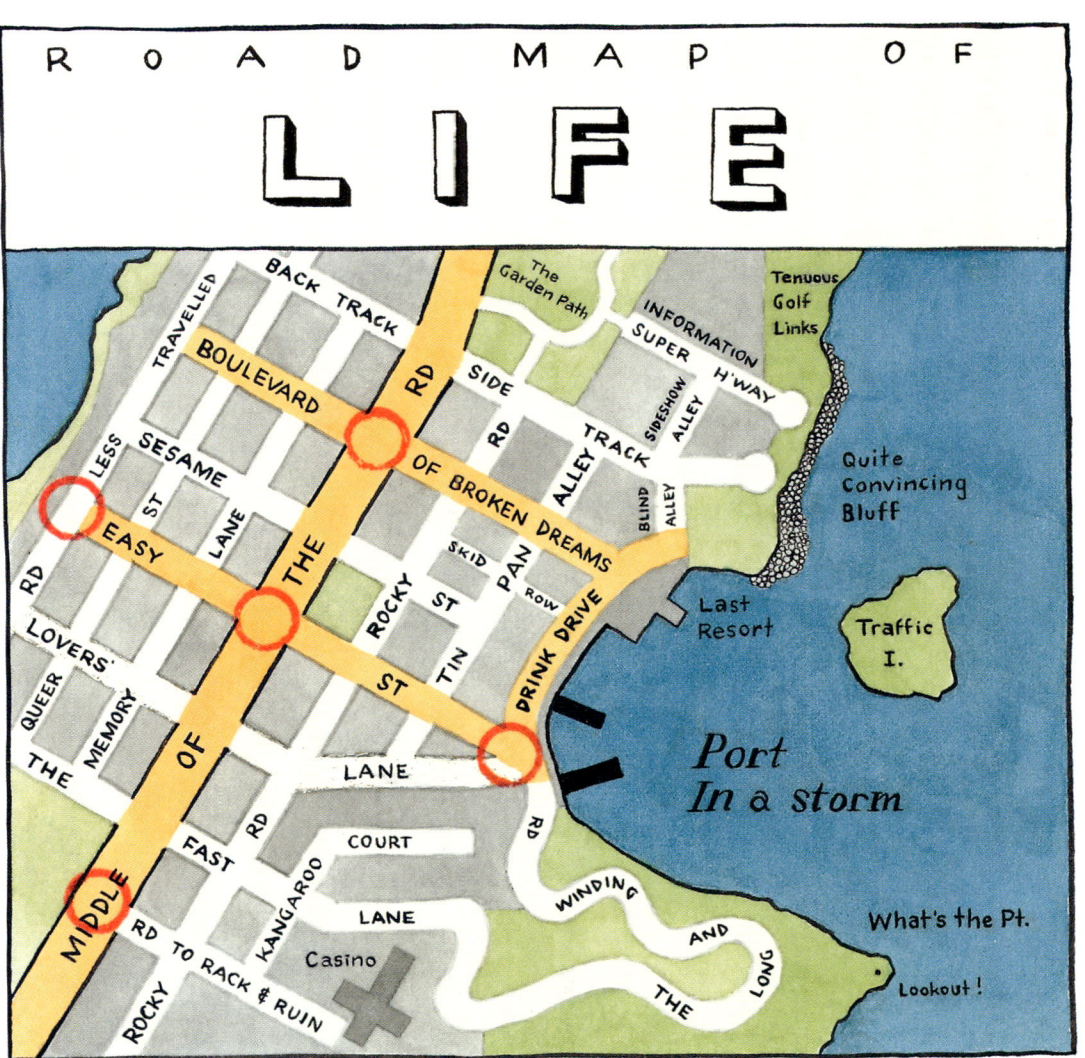

Father, what does 'share' mean?

It means; one of the equal fractional parts into which the capital stock of a limited company is divided

The ORIGINS of NED KELLY'S HEADWEAR

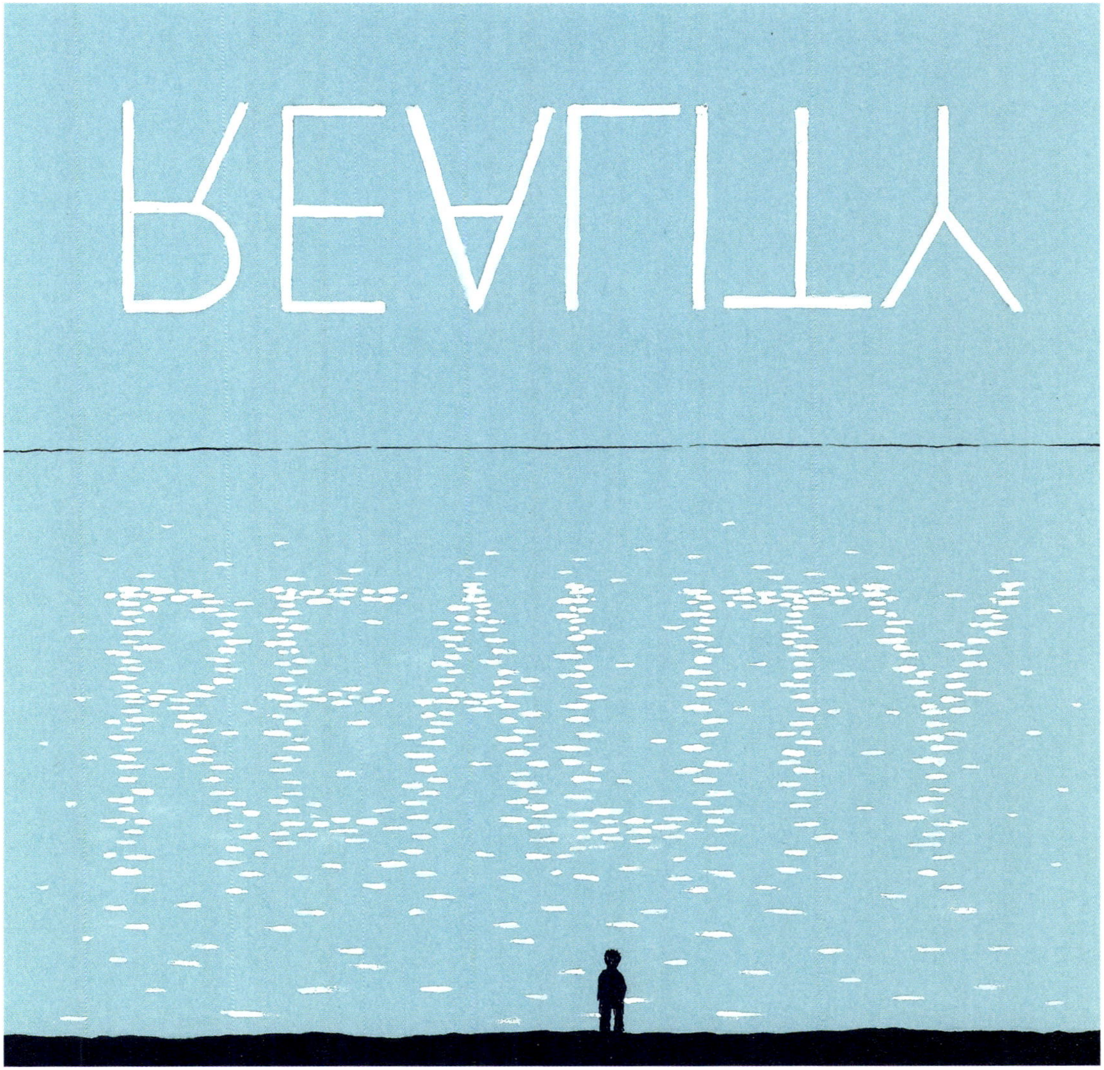
REALITY

Sure it's a nice neighbourhood... But just don't block anyone's view or you'll get yourself killed

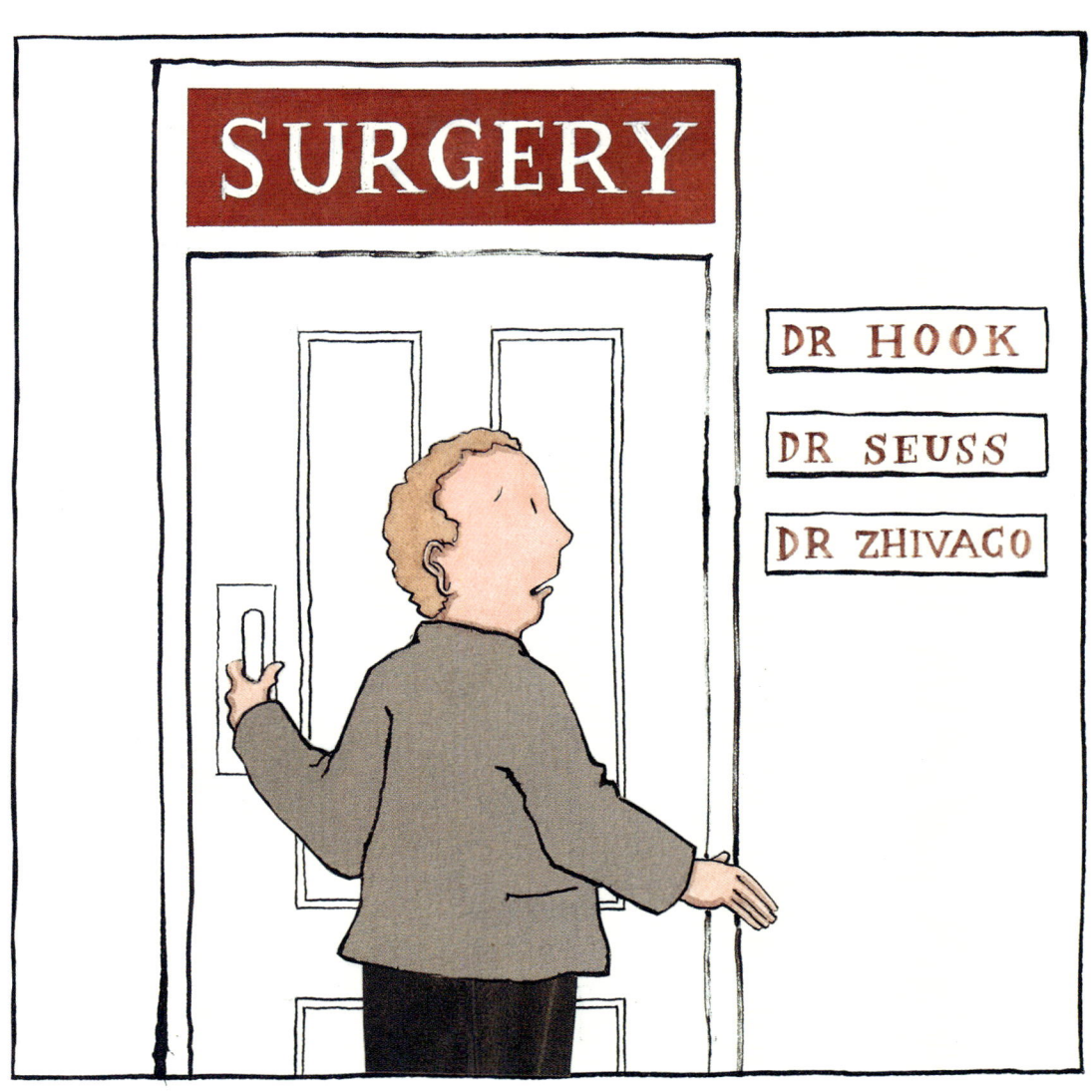

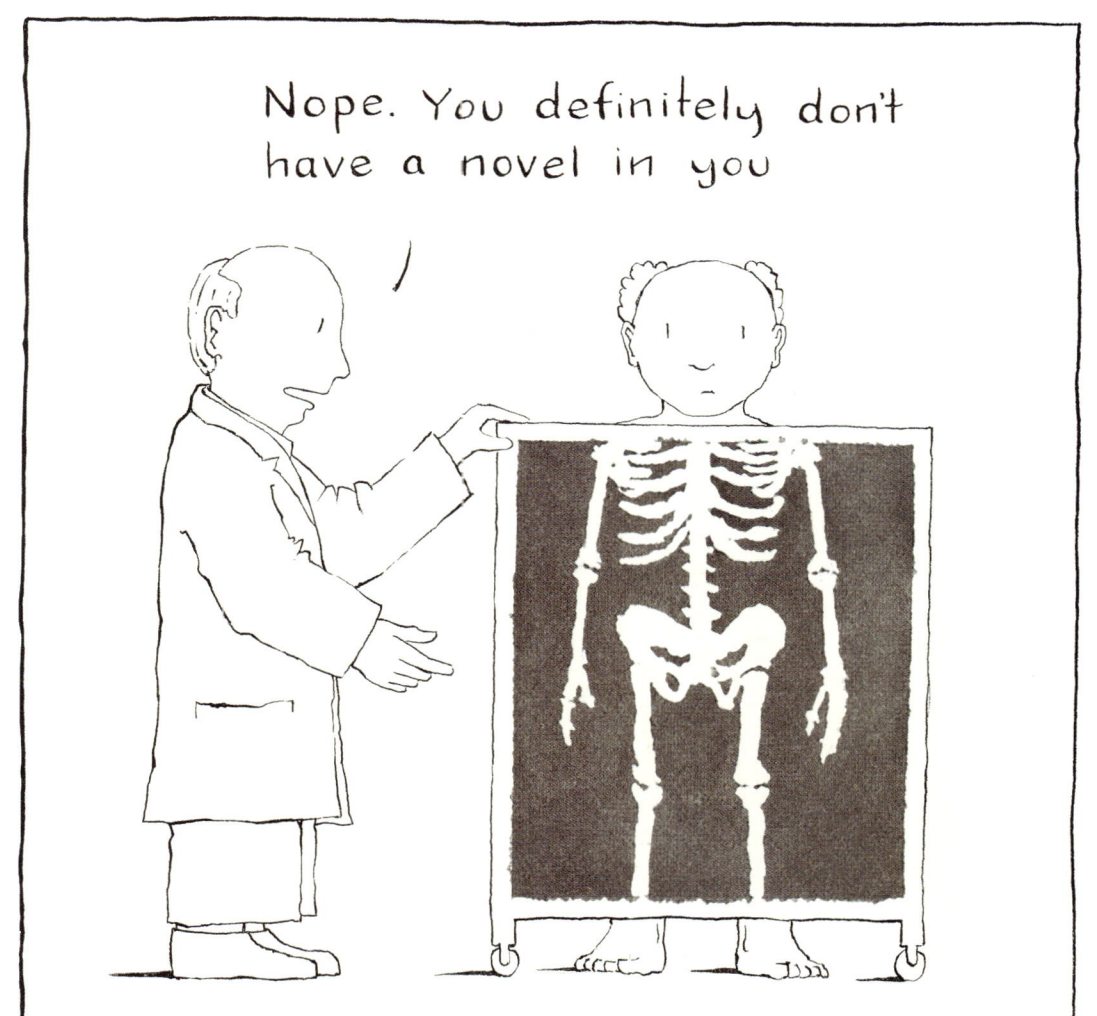

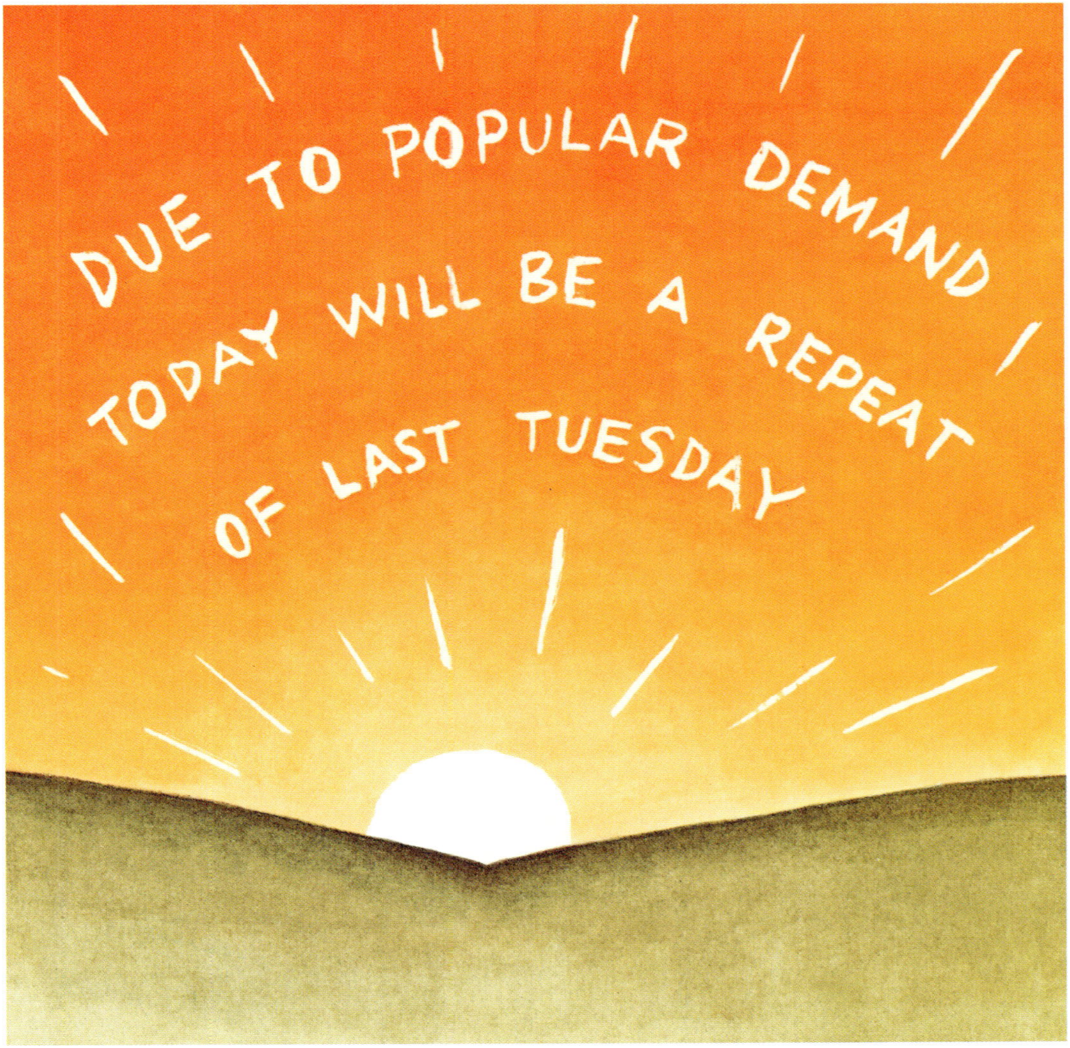
DUE TO POPULAR DEMAND
TODAY WILL BE A REPEAT
OF LAST TUESDAY

About the Author

'Tohby knits well but is also a chatterbox, so his socks are not finished. I hope he completes them in the holidays.'

Many years have passed since this mixed primary school report on Tohby Riddle. And although his socks remain unfinished, he *has* been able to complete other undertakings, including a degree in art and a degree in architecture – neither of which involved any knitting.

Tohby Riddle is also the award-winning creator of internationally published picture books such as *The Singing Hat*, *The Great Escape from City Zoo* and the cult favourite, *The Royal Guest*.

What's the Big Idea? is Tohby's first collection of cartoons. The cartoons first appeared before a wide audience in *Good Weekend* – the weekend magazine of the *Sydney Morning Herald* and Melbourne's *The Age*. Some of the cartoons have also been hung in the National Museum of Australia.

Tohby Riddle lives in Sydney, Australia.

www.tohby.com

Viking

Published by the Penguin Group
Penguin Books Australia Ltd
250 Camberwell Road
Camberwell, Victoria 3124, Australia
Penguin Books Ltd
80 Strand, London WC2R ORL, England
Penguin Putnam Inc.
375 Hudson Street, New York, New York 10014, USA
Penguin Books, a division of Pearson Canada
10 Alcorn Avenue, Toronto, Ontario, Canada M4V 3B2
Penguin Books (N.Z.) Ltd
Cnr Rosedale and Airborne Roads, Albany, Auckland, New Zealand
Penguin Books (South Africa) (Pty) Ltd
24 Sturdee Avenue, Rosebank, Johannesburg 2196, South Africa
Penguin Books India (P) Ltd
11, Community Centre, Panchsheel Park, New Delhi, 110 017, India

First published by Penguin Books Australia, 2003

1 3 5 7 9 10 8 6 4 2

Text and illustrations copyright © Tohby Riddle, 2003

The moral right of the author/illustrator has been asserted

Designed by Deborah Brash and Tohby Riddle
Typeset in 13/18pt Caslon Antique
Printed and bound by Imago Productions, Singapore Ltd.

National Library of Australia
Cataloguing-in-Publication data:

Riddle, Tohby.
What's the big idea?

ISBN 0 670 04114 9.

1. Caricatures and cartoons. I. Title.

741.59

www.penguin.com.au